99

MICHELLE KWAN

MICHELLE KWAN

CHAMPION ON ICE

Kimberly Gatto

Lerner Publications Company • Minneapolis

For my mom, Ann Gatto—Thanks for always believing in me.

To Michelle Kwan—Thanks for being such a wonderful role model to millions of people throughout the world.

Special thanks to Linda Bao and Christine deGracia for sharing their time and knowledge. Also thanks to Hilary Penlington, Anita Wong, and Douglas Jackson for their support along the way.

This book is available in two editions:
Library binding by Lerner Publications Company
Soft cover by First Avenue Editions
241 First Avenue North, Minneapolis, Minnesota 55401

Website address: www.lernerbooks.com

Library of Congress Cataloging-in-Publication Data

Gatto, Kimberly.
    Michelle Kwan : champion on ice / Kimberly Gatto.
      p. cm.
    Includes bibliographical references (p.) and index.
    Summary: A biography of the young Chinese-American figure skater who won National and World Championships in 1996 and a silver medal at the 1998 Winter Olympics.
    ISBN 0–8225–3669–2 (hardcover : alk. paper). — ISBN 0–8225–9830–2 (pbk. : alk. paper)
    1. Kwan, Michelle, 1980–   —Juvenile literature. 2. Skaters—United States—Biography—Juvenile literature. 3. Women skaters—United States—Biography—Juvenile literature. [1. Kwan, Michelle, 1980–   . 2. Ice skaters. 3. Chinese Americans—Biography. 4. Women—Biography.] I. Title.
GV850.K93G38   1998
796.91'2'092—dc21
   [b]
                                          98–16846

Manufactured in the United States of America
1 2 3 4 5 6 – JR – 03 02 01 00 99 98

Contents

Having Fun

Michelle Kwan skated onto the ice at the CoreStates Center in Philadelphia. Her heart thumped with excitement. As the music began, Michelle gazed out onto the faces of the crowd. Many were smiling. Some people waved brightly colored signs while others chanted, "We love you, Michelle." The 17-year-old figure skater took a deep breath. The crowd's admiration warmed her heart.

The sounds of "Lyra Angelica" (Song of the Angels), whispered through the arena as Michelle began her opening steps at the 1998 National Championships. Michelle had chosen "Lyra Angelica" especially for this Olympic season. The music reflected her deep love of skating. It also reminded her of her longtime dream— to represent her country at the Olympic Games.

Michelle had performed beautifully in the **technical program,** or short program. She had earned

7

seven 6.0s—perfect scores—for presentation. No woman in the history of the U.S. Nationals had ever earned perfect scores in a short program. Michelle was in first place, but winning the championship would not be easy. The **free skate,** or long program, would count for two-thirds of her final score.

The skaters draw numbers to decide the order in which they skate. Michelle would be one of the last to compete. She would have to skate cleanly to remain in the lead.

A little more than one year earlier, no one could have pictured Michelle anywhere but on top. She had been the National Champion, the World Champion, and the winner of nine straight competitions. Then came a period of self doubt. Michelle was growing up. Her body was changing, which made landing her jumps more difficult. She lost her national title, her world title, and along with those, much of her self-confidence. And as Michelle began to adjust to her losses, she suffered a stress fracture in the second toe of her left foot. This kept her in a cast—and off the ice—for a month. She didn't compete for two months.

As Michelle began her free skate at Nationals, she thought about all of these things. How can I do this if I haven't done it in two months, Michelle worried to herself. Then she put all doubts out of her head. She remembered her parents' advice: Work hard, be yourself, and have fun.

Michelle's performance to "Lyra Angelica" took first at the U.S. Nationals and second at the Olympics in 1998.

Dressed in a sky blue velvet costume, Michelle performed a breathtaking series of moves. Her program was filled with difficult footwork, jumps, spirals and spins. Michelle did each move perfectly. She made all of her jumps, even the difficult **triple lutz,** look easy. She was skating so peacefully that she did not even notice the pain in her toe. When the music ended and Michelle left the ice, several of the judges and many of the viewers were in tears.

"When I went out on the ice," she later explained, "I saw all the signs and heard people yell, 'We love you, Michelle,' and I wanted to melt right there on the ice. I just listened to my music. I thought of clouds, I thought of angels."

Michelle hugged Frank Carroll, her coach. Together they watched the nine judges' scores being posted. The first set of scores, for technical merit, measured how well she had completed the required elements, like jumps and spins. These marks were very high. Next came the scores for presentation. Eight 6.0s flashed upon the board. Not only had Michelle won the National title, but she had made figure skating history. Never before had any skater received eight 6.0s in a long program at the Nationals. "The key to pulling that off," Michelle later said, "was to just have fun. And I did."

Michelle accepted her gold medal, and she earned the honor of leading her team to the Olympics.

Coach Carroll and Michelle see her Nationals scores.

Six weeks after Nationals, Michelle traveled to the Japanese city of Nagano (NAH-gah-noh) to compete in the Olympic Games. Her toe had still not healed, but Michelle didn't make any excuses. She skated two beautiful, clean programs, winning the short program and placing second in the long. But Michelle's teammate, Tara Lipinski, won the gold medal with a stunning performance in the long program. Michelle earned the silver. Many fans were disappointed that Michelle had not won the gold. "I didn't lose the gold medal," Michelle said, "I won the silver." She had worked hard, she'd been herself, and most of all, she'd had fun. And that, for Michelle, is what skating is all about.

By the time she was 13, Michelle had been taking skating lessons for more than six years.

The Dream Begins

Michelle Kwan was born on July 7, 1980, in Torrance, California, a suburb of Los Angeles. She was the third child born to Danny and Estella Kwan. Danny named Michelle after the title of his favorite Beatles song. Michelle has an older brother, Ron, and an older sister, Karen. Ron is a student at the University of California at Irvine. Karen, who attends Boston University, is also a talented figure skater. Michelle and Karen sometimes compete against each other.

Michelle's parents came to the United States from Hong Kong in the early 1970s. Estella was born in Hong Kong. Danny's family lived in Guangzhou (Canton), China. Danny and Estella had first met during their school days, but they did not fall in love until many years later.

The Kwans are a very close family. They are also hardworking. Danny Kwan's family was poor. He began working when he was just 13. When he was 22, he visited California for a wedding and decided to move there. Danny worked for Pacific Bell, a Los Angeles telephone company, for many years.

While Danny was earning a living in California, Estella worked as a nurse and then as a TV news anchor in Hong Kong. When Danny returned to Hong Kong for a school reunion, he and Estella fell in love. They married and moved to California. Danny also worked in the family's restaurant, The Golden Pheasant, which Estella managed.

One day, while watching brother Ron practice hockey, Karen decided that she wanted to learn how to figure skate. So did Michelle. At first, Danny and Estella thought their tiny daughter was too young. But Michelle persisted until they gave in. Both girls began taking group lessons at the local rink, which was located in a shopping mall in Rancho Palos Verdes. "My first skating memory is from when I was six," says Michelle. "I was wearing rental skates and eating Nerds candy."

Michelle and Karen began their skating careers wearing rented brown skates that hurt their feet. The girls didn't care. They loved being on the ice. At first, they held onto the boards at the side of the rink for balance. Once they could stand alone, the girls learned to glide across the ice. They also learned to skate backwards. This is an important skill for a figure skater because all of the jumps except for the **axel** are attempted from a backward position. The axel is named for its inventor, Axel Paulsen, and it is the toughest jump of all.

When their family could afford it, Michelle and Karen took private lessons with coach Derek James. With James, they learned more difficult moves. Michelle loved learning new jumps. Her small body could rotate quickly in the air. But learning new things is never easy. Like all skaters, Michelle often ended up on the cold, hard ice. Yet each time she fell, she got up and tried again.

Michelle with her parents, Estella and Danny

Michelle and her sister, Karen, share a love for figure skating.

Being on the ice with Karen made skating even more fun for Michelle. The girls got to spend lots of time together. Their friends at the rink called Michelle "Little Kwan." Karen, who was taller and two years older, was known as "Big Kwan." Both Michelle and Karen loved to skate and they soon became good skaters.

As they improved, Michelle and Karen began entering local competitions. The United States Figure Skating Association (USFSA) sponsors tests and competitions throughout the country. Events are broken down into skill levels. The basic level is pre-preliminary. After completing the moves for that level, a skater may move up to the preliminary, pre-juvenile, juvenile, intermediate, novice, junior, and senior ranks. Olympic-level competitors skate at the senior level.

Michelle won her first gold medal when she was only seven years old. That's when her Olympic dream began. She watched on television as Brian Boitano captured the gold for the United States. Boitano's skating was so magical that he seemed to tell a story through his moves. Michelle wanted to perform like that. She remembered, "I thought, OK, tomorrow I will go to the Olympics."

Michelle worked hard toward her goal of skating in the Olympics. She rarely missed a practice. She skated every single day, even when she was tired, cold, or sick. She even practiced on Christmas Day! Michelle's efforts soon paid off. In 1990, she missed only two of her jumps during an entire season of competitions. Little Kwan's persistence and winning outlook had put her far above other skaters.

Michelle's skating career really took off in 1993.

3

A Big Step

Michelle's grandmother had given her a very special gift. It was a gold charm with a dragon, the Chinese symbol for good luck. Michelle treasured this gift. The sparkling pendant is around her neck each time Michelle takes to the ice.

With her dragon pendant on a pretty red cord, Michelle felt blessed with luck. Yet the Kwans knew that it would take more than luck for Michelle to become an Olympic skater. Very few skaters ever make it that far. Skating at the senior level would take years of hard work and extraordinary talent. On top of that, lessons and ice time cost money.

Danny Kwan told his daughters that he would support them fully in their skating if that's what they really wanted to do. But the girls would have to make some sacrifices. There would not be enough money for new clothes or skates. Michelle and Karen would have to wear hand-me-downs. They saved their change in an empty watercooler bottle. Everyone in the Kwan family—Danny, Estella, and Ron—helped the girls.

By the time Michelle was 11, she was skating very well. Even without a full-time coach, Michelle was already competing in junior events. She won a gold medal at the 1992 Southwest Pacific Regionals and a bronze at the Pacific Coast Sectionals. That third-place finish qualified her for the Junior National Championships. There she would face the most talented young skaters in the entire country. Skating was no longer just a hobby for Michelle.

That year, Michelle's skating caught the attention of many people, including Frank Carroll. Carroll is one of the best coaches in the world. He had already guided many skaters to world and national titles. Olympic silver medalist Linda Fratianne and national champion Christopher Bowman were just two of his many famous pupils.

Coach Carroll worked at the Ice Castle Training Center in Lake Arrowhead, a few hours away from Torrance. This top-notch skating facility, high up in the California mountains, had everything a skater could want. At first, Michelle and Karen traveled there for lessons every weekend. Then, the Ice Castle Foundation offered them scholarships to train full-time. The Foundation would pay all of their expenses!

This lucky pendant was a gift from Michelle's grandmother.

The girls would have to move to Lake Arrowhead, however. They would have to leave their home, their school, and their friends behind.

Danny Kwan went with Michelle and Karen to Lake Arrowhead. The three moved into a small cabin called "Debi Thomas Teepee," named for the 1988 Olympic bronze medalist. Each day, Danny drove more than 100 miles to and from work. He made sure he was home in plenty of time to tuck the girls into bed at night. Estella and Ron stayed behind in Torrance, but visited often.

Michelle and Karen loved living at Ice Castle. They went to school with other skaters at the Ice Castle lodge.

Coach Carroll teaches Michelle at the Ice Castle facility.

Best of all, they shared the rink with some of the top figure skaters in the world. Sometimes they trained with skaters they had seen on television!

Coach Carroll was strict when he needed to be, but he was also soft-spoken and kind. He said that with training, Michelle could become one of the top junior skaters in the world. But Michelle had had enough of junior skating. She wanted to compete with the senior skaters—mature, elegant young women like Kristi Yamaguchi, Lu Chen, and Nancy Kerrigan.

To compete in the senior ranks, a skater must perform a series of moves before a panel of judges. Skaters call this the "gold test." Despite the difficult jumps required, Michelle felt certain that she could pass the gold test. But when she asked her coach's permission to try, he firmly said no. At the Junior Nationals that year, she had placed ninth. Coach Carroll wanted Michelle to gain more experience before she competed in senior events.

Michelle would not take "no" for an answer. She waited until her coach was out of town at a coaches' conference. Then she asked her dad to drive her to take the test. Danny Kwan asked Michelle if Coach Carroll had given her permission to take the test. Michelle mumbled her answer to her father. Danny thought she had said "yes," but really she had mumbled "no." Michelle had never lied to her parents. Danny drove Michelle to the test, which she passed with flying colors. Michelle was a senior lady!

When Coach Carroll returned, he was angry. "He was steaming," said Michelle. "His eyes were bugging out." But there was no turning back. According to USFSA rules, once a skater has passed the gold test, she must compete in senior events. Michelle could skate in the World Junior Championships because of her age, but after that she would have to compete as a senior.

To Coach Carroll's surprise, Michelle skated better as a senior than she had as a junior. That year she won four events, including her first international competition, the Gardena Spring Trophy in Italy. In January 1993, Michelle became the youngest competitor in the ladies' senior Nationals since Priscilla Hill had skated in 1973. Wearing a pair of borrowed skates, Michelle performed well enough to place sixth. She taped a fortune cookie message into her scrapbook. The message read: "You are entering a time of great promise and overdue rewards."

Months later, Michelle set her first figure skating record. At the Olympic Festival, in San Antonio, Texas, Michelle became the youngest festival champion. She performed in front of 25,691 people—the largest crowd ever for a skating event. In October, *Skating* magazine put Michelle's photo on its cover.

That winter, Michelle skated in the World Junior Championships, in Colorado. Although she had been competing as a senior, Michelle was allowed to skate in the World Junior Championships. This competition took Michelle one step closer to her Olympic dream. Many Olympic medalists, including Kristi Yamaguchi and Paul Wylie, had won the World Junior title.

A happy Michelle
celebrates her World
Junior Championship.

Michelle completed a series of dazzling triple jumps to win the short program at the Junior Worlds. In the free skate, she missed her triple **loop** by rotating once instead of the required three times in the air. Michelle knew that the judges would have to take away points for that, but she did not let the mistake distract her. She skated faster and stronger and completed five more triples in near-perfect form. The judges placed her in first. Michelle Kwan was the World Junior Champion!

As a senior skater, Michelle competed against the best female figure skaters in the world.

4

Rising Star

As the 1994 Olympics approached, everyone at Ice Castle was excited. Michelle was excited, too. Although she was just 13, she dreamed of competing at the 1994 Games. The United States could only send two women to the Olympics. Nancy Kerrigan, the 1992 Olympic bronze medalist, was the favorite for the Olympic team. Kerrigan's main rival was Tonya Harding, a skater known for her jumping ability. Harding was the first U.S. woman—and the second in the world—to perform a triple axel in a competition.

In January 1994, Michelle went to Detroit for her second senior Nationals. As the skaters entered Cobo Hall for practice, a man clubbed Kerrigan on the knee. Michelle heard the attack. "People were going, 'Nancy, Nancy, I want your autograph,'" she told a reporter. "So I let her go ahead of me. And just as she walked through the curtain, I heard a big scream."

Kerrigan was on the floor, crying in pain. Skaters, coaches and fans were scared. They could not imagine why someone would attack a skater. Later, police found out that Tonya Harding's husband and her bodyguard had planned the attack. Police and figure skating officials wondered if Harding herself had been involved.

Kerrigan's knee was so badly injured that she could not compete at Nationals. Harding easily won the title. As the National Champion, she got the first place on the U.S. Olympic team. Meanwhile, Michelle outperformed the other skaters to win the silver medal. Normally, a second-place finish would have earned Michelle a spot on the Olympic team. But because Kerrigan had done well at the last Olympics, skating officials saved the second spot on the team for her.

The U.S. Olympic Committee had a lot of questions. What if Kerrigan's knee did not heal in time for the Olympics? What if Harding had been involved in the attack? The U.S. team needed an alternate skater, and a good one.

Michelle had won the World Junior title and a silver at Nationals. The U.S. Olympic Committee members felt confident that she would be the best choice to step in if Kerrigan or Harding couldn't compete at the Olympics.

If Michelle got to compete, she would be the youngest U.S. Olympian in history. She was only 13.

Michelle's youthful enthusiasm spiced her routines.

Kerrigan and Harding were both in their 20s! Everyone wanted to interview Michelle. Reporters talked to her parents. Some reporters camped outside the Ice Castle rink. Lawyers offered to sue the U.S. Olympic Committee if Michelle was not allowed to compete in Harding's place. The Kwans refused.

In mid-February 1994, Michelle, her dad, and Coach Carroll flew to Norway for the Olympic Games. As the team's alternate, Michelle was not invited inside the Olympic village. She wasn't even allowed to practice with the other skaters. But Michelle had to be ready to represent her country if Kerrigan or Harding were unable to skate. "I have to keep training and stay focused in case I'm asked to compete," Michelle told a *Chicago Tribune* reporter.

As she skated against older skaters, Michelle added more dramatic movements to her routines.

But Michelle wasn't asked to skate. Both Kerrigan and Harding competed in the Olympic Games. Kerrigan won a silver medal for the United States. Harding missed her triple axel and finished in eighth place. Oksana Baiul, a 16-year-old from the Ukraine, won the gold.

Throughout the competition, Michelle cheered loudly for her teammates. She was happy that Kerrigan had been able to compete, even though it meant that Michelle could not. "When I was watching, I wanted to go and get out of my jeans and put my skating clothes on and just go out there," she said. "But I was happy being there and just being at the Olympics was an honor."

After returning home from Norway, Michelle was chosen to compete at the World Championships in Chiba, Japan. Kerrigan had chosen not to take part, and Harding was facing legal problems. Michelle and 16-year-old Nicole Bobek were the U.S. team.

Michelle skated well in her qualifying round, placing fifth among the world's top skaters. Bobek did not do well in the qualifying and was cut from the competition. Michelle felt the pressure of being the United States's only skater during her short program. She finished in 11th place.

Michelle bounced back the following day with a brilliant free skate. Her performance to "East of Eden" was packed with triple jumps. She moved up from 11th to 8th overall. Because Michelle placed in the top 10, the United States would be allowed to send two women to the next year's Worlds. Kristi Yamaguchi, the 1992 Olympic gold medalist, told reporters: "I am very impressed. Given her age, it's incredible what she's accomplished."

Michelle returned to California more determined than ever. She knew that with practice, she would keep getting better. Michelle no longer attended school. She studied with a tutor in between her skating practices.

"You really have to have quality time and outline your schedule well," Michelle said. "When you are doing homework, you can't be doing it partially. When you skate, you can't think about anything else."

Michelle did exceptionally well in both her schoolwork and her skating that season. She won the U.S. Ladies' Outdoor Challenge and placed second in the Goodwill Games and at Skate America. In some events, she and Karen competed against each other. "I actually think it's fun and interesting," Michelle said of their rivalry. On and off the ice, Michelle and Karen are close, as sisters and best friends.

Along with Karen, Michelle had lots of friends at Lake Arrowhead. She also kept in touch with many of her school friends from Torrance. "We write letters," she says. "I have pen pals . . . from third grade and first grade. And I do a lot of things with my friends up at Ice Castle."

Michelle spent the summer of 1994 with the Tour of World Figure Skating Champions (TOC). The annual three-month tour stops in more than 60 cities throughout the United States, such as Boston and Chicago. Thirteen-year-old Michelle was the youngest performer on the tour. Michelle's mom traveled with her.

Michelle was thrilled to be with the world's top skaters. She learned by watching them perform each night. Backstage, she played Ping-Pong with world champions Elvis Stojko (STOY-coh) and Lu Chen.

Although she was younger than many of the skaters on the Tour of Champions, Michelle enjoyed herself.

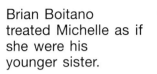

Brian Boitano treated Michelle as if she were his younger sister.

She joked with Olympic champ Brian Boitano. Stojko and Boitano became like brothers to Michelle, giving her pointers on technique and jumps. They helped her learn the triple axel. Boitano gave Michelle the nickname "Shelley," which the other skaters on the tour began using as well.

That year, the readers of *Skating* magazine voted for Michelle as Skater of the Year. The magazine hosted a banquet for Michelle and presented her with a beautiful award. Michelle was the youngest skater ever to receive this award.

By the time the 1995 Nationals arrived, Michelle was the hands-down favorite to win. Both American skaters who had challenged her the previous year were gone. Kerrigan had turned **professional.** Harding had admitted to participating in the attack on Kerrigan. The USFSA banned her from any of its events. Michelle's main contender, Nicole Bobek, had been having trouble landing her jumps.

But, as Michelle would say, nothing is certain in skating. At Nationals, Bobek performed a nearly perfect long program. Then it was Michelle's turn. After starting out strong, she stumbled on her final jump, a triple lutz, and fell to the ice. That mistake cost her the National title. Michelle had hoped to win, but she knew that Bobek deserved the gold.

After her free skate, Michelle and her coach went to the waiting area to watch for the scores. Skaters call that place the "kiss and cry" area because skaters usually kiss their coach and cry while receiving their scores. As she waited for her marks, Michelle saw something slide down the floor toward her feet. It was a huge heart-shaped box of candy. Michelle smiled. She knew that Harris Collins, a special friend of the Kwan family, had sent the box.

Harris was the brother of Tom Collins, the manager of the Tour of Champions. A kindhearted and funny man, Harris Collins always tried to make young skaters feel more confident while they were away from home. "The first year, I didn't know anybody," said Michelle. "Harris was always there for me. He made me laugh."

After Nationals, Michelle traveled to Birmingham, England, for her second World Championships. Michelle's free skate included a triple lutz–**double** toe **combination,** which earned four marks of 5.9. Two of the judges placed her first! Michelle finished fourth at the championships, just a spot short of winning a medal. "I knew I skated my best," Michelle said. "It was so overwhelming. All the American flags waving. Everyone standing. It was so incredible."

The audience could not get enough of Michelle. The fans gave her a full standing ovation. Many threw flowers and gifts onto the ice. Michelle had already received hundreds of stuffed animals from her fans. There were too many to fit in her room, and she wanted other youngsters to be able to enjoy them. Michelle came up with an idea. She would give the stuffed animals to patients at Los Angeles Children's Hospital. Michelle enjoyed giving away the toys so much that she made it a regular project. When a new skating rink opened near the hospital, Michelle gave skating lessons to many of the children.

Michelle spent her second summer on the TOC tour, where she skated to music from *Peter Pan.* After the tour, Michelle performed in a televised special called "Too Hot to Skate." The show was filmed near the boardwalk in Santa Cruz, California. In a navy blue bathing suit and matching baseball cap, Michelle had a blast skating to the Beach Boys song, "California Girls."

Fans shower Michelle with flowers and stuffed animals.

Her pal, Elvis Stojko, held a jumping contest near the sand. Nancy Kerrigan threw beach balls into the audience while she skated. Everyone had a lot of fun.

Back home at Ice Castle, Michelle and Coach Carroll began working on her programs for the new season. Coach Carroll thought that Michelle had not won a senior Worlds medal because she still looked like a junior skater. Her youthful jumps were fun to watch, but the judges wanted more ladylike elegance.

Coach Carroll and Lori Nichol created the **choreography** for a free skate routine for Michelle. The music they chose told the story of Salome, the stepdaughter of King Herod Antipas. According to biblical stories, Salome danced for the king in return for the head of John the Baptist. Michelle would have to be more than just a skater. She would have to become an actress on the ice.

5

On Top of the World

As Michelle developed in her skating, she learned to perform with drama and emotion. In skating, this is called artistry. Michelle had to convey to the audience and to the judges exactly what Salome must have been feeling. For Michelle, it was like being an actor or ballerina. Michelle also had to wear lots of lipstick and mascara. "I was afraid to jump with mascara on," Michelle jokingly told reporters.

Coach Carroll hoped that Michelle's new look would catch the attention of the judges. It did. At Skate America, the first competition of the season, some onlookers did not even recognize Michelle. Some of the change was because of the makeup. The biggest change, however, was the emotion that Michelle had added to her skating. She showed the judges all the passion and love that she had for skating. Michelle bested a field of incredible skaters, including the Chinese skater Lu Chen, the reigning World Champion. The day Michelle won the gold medal at Skate America was her dad's birthday.

Going into the 1996 Nationals, Michelle was once again favored to win. This time, she came through. Karen also skated beautifully and placed fifth. "My happiest moment wasn't when I won the gold," Michelle later said. "It was when I saw Karen skate so well." Karen was thrilled to see her little sister become a champion.

After Nationals came the World Championships in Edmonton, Canada. For the third time, Michelle would go head-to-head with the reigning champ, Lu Chen, who is known as "Lulu" to her friends. Skating to an elegant Spanish medley called *Romanza*, Michelle edged out Lulu in the short program. But the free skate, Lulu's strength, was still to come.

By draw, Lulu skated before Michelle. The Chinese champion was flawless. As she performed, Michelle and her coach found a quiet place backstage. Far behind the curtains and stands, Coach Carroll gave Michelle a pep talk. Nothing could drown out the applause for Lulu's marks, which included two 6.0s for presentation. Lulu's was a tough act to follow. Michelle would have to be perfect to win.

As soon as she glided onto the ice, Michelle transported the crowd to another world. Every jump was perfect. Every move was soft and flowing. Toward the end of her free skate, Michelle thought she needed to add something. After completing a lovely **sit spin,** she added a triple loop. The fans leapt to their feet. People shouted, "Six! Six!" As Michelle said later, "It was the World Championships, and I skated the very best of my life."

Michelle's coach was thrilled. So were her parents. The judges had a tough decision to make. Both Lulu and Michelle had skated wonderfully.

When Michelle's marks were posted, she received two 6.0s also. Michelle's performance as Salome won first-place votes from six of the nine judges. With those marks, she became the world champion. Lu Chen won the silver medal, and Irina Slutskaya (SLOOT-sky-ah) of Russia took the bronze.

Irina Slutskaya, Michelle, and Lu Chen at the 1996 Worlds

Michelle, the 15-year-old world champion, won almost every competition she entered that year. She captured gold at Skate America, Skate Canada and the Nation's Cup. She topped that string off with a win at the Champions Series Final. Michelle's only defeat of the season was a third-place finish at the Centennial Cup in Russia. That day, she had the flu.

Besides being one of the world's best skaters, Michelle had become one of the most popular. Fans appreciated the time she spent signing autographs and chatting with them. They voted for her as *Skating* magazine's Skater of the Year. She became the only two-time winner of the award. Michelle also appeared on *The Late Show with David Letterman* and was invited to visit the White House.

Michelle also found time to help others. She joined the Children's Miracle Network (CMN), a charity that raises money for sick children. Michelle and other celebrity sponsors, like San Francisco quarterback Steve Young and gymnast Mary Lou Retton, helped raise money for CMN.

By the summer of 1996, Michelle was back in the Tour of Champions. She had an exciting new **exhibition** number. In this routine, Michelle skated to "Just Around the Riverbend" from the hit Disney movie, *Pocahontas.* With her long black hair flowing in the wind, she looked a lot like an Indian princess. "Except I wear skates," she often joked.

Michelle performs as the Indian princess Pocahontas.

One evening in June, while the tour was in Chicago, Harris Collins suddenly collapsed. "We were in the dressing room and didn't know what happened," said Michelle. "We were very scared. As we were skating, we were praying." Harris Collins died later that evening.

Harris Collins was a friend to Michelle and many other skaters.

Harris had been one of Michelle's best friends on the tour. She wanted to do something to celebrate his life. She decided to skate a program in his memory. She choreographed a routine to the song "Winter," performed by Tori Amos. "It reminds me of skating and I know how much he loved skating," Michelle said.

In the fall, Michelle and her parents visited Beijing, China, for a special performance of the show *Cinderella On Ice.* Michelle played the title role on opening night. She was thrilled to skate in China, the homeland of her parents and grandparents.

Later, Michelle won gold medals at Skate America and Trophee Lalique. Her final victory of 1996 was at the Ultimate Four Challenge in Boston, Massachusetts. Professionals compete against amateurs in this event. Michelle was excited and a little nervous about competing against Kristi Yamaguchi and World Professional Champion Yuka Sato.

44

Michelle was in second place after the short program, but her flawless performance of *Pocahontas* won the free skate and the championship.

The Kwans made sure that Michelle didn't develop a swelled head, despite all her victories. They often tease her about flunking her driving test. "I was so nervous," Michelle says. "Even more than I was at the Worlds. I did really bad. I mean, oh, yuck." On the second try, Michelle passed the test.

Michelle dedicated her performance to the song "Winter" to the memory of her friend Harris.

Her bubbly personality delights Michelle's fans.

6

Always a Champion

Michelle had a whirlwind year as the world figure skating champion. Yet, exciting as it was, being the best was not easy. The more Michelle won, the more pressure she felt. People began to call her "invincible."

Michelle had set a record by winning 12 of her last 13 competitions. Heading into the 1997 Nationals, everyone thought that she would win. Nobody was surprised when Michelle won the short program, skating to "Dream of Desdemona."

Michelle's free skate music, "Taj Mahal," told the story of a beautiful Indian goddess. Michelle looked the part in her elegant red costume and sash. As the music played, Michelle soared into a beautiful triple lutz. Perfect. Her **toe loop** combination was coming up. Michelle seemed calm and confident. But after easily landing the first element, she lost her balance and fell. The audience gasped.

Michelle stumbles during the U.S. Nationals free skate.

Michelle picked herself up and headed into her next jump, a triple **flip.** She fell again. Then she panicked. She fell a third time on her triple loop. The crowd cheered Michelle on as she completed the most difficult four minutes of her life. Tara Lipinski, the final skater to perform, moved into first place and won the title. Michelle slipped to second.

Michelle was very upset because she had skated so poorly. She began to doubt herself. Despite these worries, Michelle smiled throughout the closing ceremonies. The next day she laughed with fans and signed autographs. She even teased her family for "not congratulating her" on her silver medal. Deep inside, Michelle was scared. She was still growing up. Her body was changing, which threw off her sense of balance. Jumps that Michelle had once landed easily were becoming more difficult to do. And the World Championships were only weeks away.

Those weeks flew by. Michelle came in second behind Lipinski at the Champions Series Final. Then she traveled to Lausanne, Switzerland, to defend her World Championship crown. In the short program, Michelle stepped out of her triple lutz. That mistake put her into fourth place and virtually erased any chance she had to win the gold medal. Alone in her dressing room, Michelle cried. "I felt like a bug caught in a spider web," she later told *The New York Times*. "I was confused. I panicked."

As Michelle prepared for her free skate performance, she thought about some recent events. Carlo Fassi, a trainer at Ice Castle who coached teammate Nicole Bobek, had died after a heart attack. Skater Scott Hamilton, a close friend of Michelle's, had learned he had cancer. Michelle realized that losing her world title was not a matter of life and death. She would go out there and skate the best she could, not for a gold medal, but just for herself.

Out on the ice, Michelle skated fast and free. She landed all of her jumps and made just one mistake, turning one jump into a double instead of a triple. Michelle won the free skate. She moved up from fourth to second place in the standings. If Michelle had been just one notch higher in the short program, she would have won the world title. But Michelle did not focus on what could have been. "It's a wonderful feeling to fly again," she said. "I learned more about being a champion than any other time, when I came in second at Nationals and Worlds." Michelle had proven that she could win, and lose, with dignity.

Michelle and Tara Lipinski proudly display their medals after the 1997 World Championships.

Michelle takes time to sign autographs for her fans.

After the Worlds, Michelle appeared on *The Tonight Show*. She joked with host Jay Leno and his guests. Michelle even showed Jay how to perform a double axel on dry land! A few weeks later, Michelle was featured in a television special called *Busch Gardens and Sea World Alien Vacation*. In June, she threw out the first pitch at a Chicago White Sox–Baltimore Orioles baseball game. She also visited Orlando, Florida, where she·appeared in several segments of the Children's Miracle Network Telethon.

Michelle spent most of the spring and summer performing with the Tour of Champions. She dazzled the crowds with a new exhibition number from the musical *Les Miserables*. Michelle had chosen the music. She and Lori Nichol choreographed the routine in just one night. The audiences loved it.

In July, Brian Boitano chose Michelle to star with him in a show he directed called *Skating Romance III*. Michelle was the only non-professional skater in the show. She skated with Brian, whom she had idolized since she was a little girl, to the song "I Love Paris."

After the tour, Michelle began perfecting her new programs. She worked very hard, not only on the ice, but also training and working out at the gym every day. Michelle wanted her body to be in tip-top shape for the upcoming Olympic Games.

Michelle unveiled her new programs at Skate America in October. Reporters had spent months building up the competition as a showdown between Michelle and Tara Lipinski. Michelle made it clear that she was back on top. She easily won both the short and long programs.

Skate America was Michelle's first 1997 Champions Series event. In the Champions Series, each skater is assigned to two international events. The skaters earn points. The top six finishers go to the Champions Series Finals. Michelle was especially excited about her second series assignment—the NHK Trophy—because that event was to be held on the Olympic ice in Nagano, Japan.

Michelle performs to "On My Own" from *Les Miserables.*

The NHK Trophy was scheduled for four and half weeks after Skate America. Michelle thought that was too much time between competitions. She wanted to be out on the ice. She talked with her coach and her parents, and decided to compete in Skate Canada in November. Michelle would not earn series points for the event, but she could still compete.

Artistry and drama
are Michelle's
hallmarks.

Michelle easily won the short program at Skate Canada, but her free skate was far from dazzling. Michelle didn't have her usual spark. At the end of the program, she fell while doing a fairly easy move. Reporters asked Michelle if she hadn't skated well because her coach was not there. Michelle said only that she could have done much better. There was a big reason why Michelle had not skated so well, but she didn't want to tell anyone. The second toe on her left foot was throbbing with pain.

Despite her less-than-perfect performance, Michelle earned the gold. Then, she went home to California for some medical tests. Doctors told her that she had a stress fracture in her toe. She would need to rest, with a cast from the knee down, for two to three weeks. No triple jumps, no sit spins, no skating. And the Olympics were less than three months away.

Michelle dropped out of the NHK Trophy. The international committee decided that since she had won both Skate America and Skate Canada, she would be allowed to compete in the Champions Series Final. But when the finals rolled around, Michelle's toe still hurt.

Michelle tried to make something out of the bad experience. She worked out at the gym, wrote in her diary, and focused on her schoolwork. She told reporters that she would compete at the upcoming Nationals, even if she had to compete injured.

Michelle did return to the ice, but her toe still hurt. Certain jumps, especially the triple toe loop, hurt the most. Michelle did not practice very much because she was afraid of making the injury worse. Still, she decided to compete at Nationals. The U.S. Olympic team would be selected there, and Michelle wanted to earn her way to the Games.

When Michelle arrived at Nationals, many people wondered if she would be able to skate at all. She was still having trouble with the triple toe loop, but she substituted it for the even more difficult triple flip in her short program. Rising to the challenge, Michelle earned the highest scores in history for both programs.

Michelle's short program at the Olympics was superb, but Tara Lipinski edged her out for the gold medal.

After her stunning performance at Nationals, Michelle was the favorite for the Olympic gold medal.

At the Olympics, Michelle's artistic skating in the short program dazzled the judges. Her toe felt a lot better, and she was happy just to be skating on Olympic ice.

After the short program, the top group of skaters drew numbers to determine the starting order for the free skate. Michelle drew the first spot, the worst position. In international competitions, judges generally give low marks at first, so that there is room to give higher marks to the other competitors. Most skaters would rather skate later in the competition.

Skating to "Lyra Angelica," Michelle performed a clean and elegant program. Her presentation scores were all 5.9s but her technical marks were lower. The scores were good enough for the top spot, but there was room for another skater to slip into first.

That was just what Tara Lipinski did. Skating next to last, Lipinski performed the most technically difficult program of the evening. Her technical marks moved her into first. Michelle had to settle for the silver medal.

Michelle was disappointed but she acted like a champion. She congratulated Lipinski many times, and said how happy she was just to be at the Games. Michelle's sportsmanship pleased her fans and won her new ones. When she appeared on *The Tonight Show* a week after the Olympics, Michelle received a standing ovation. Host Jay Leno called Michelle "a true American hero."

The medalists: Lu Chen, Tara Lipinski and Michelle

Michelle is sure to get even more fan letters than the more than 200 letters a week she was receiving before the Olympics. That will make answering each letter even more difficult. "I try to keep up with it," she says, "because I know how much people appreciate it."

Although she spends most of her time on the ice, Michelle kept a straight "A" average during high school. As a senior, she won the Dial Award, a scholarship given to the top high school athlete in America.

Michelle enjoys skating for medals, but she says that winning isn't everything. Happiness is spending time with family and friends—shopping, riding roller coasters, and fishing. Once, while on tour in Alaska, Michelle went fishing with Todd Eldredge and Lloyd Eisler. The other skaters went home empty-handed but Michelle caught a 25-pound salmon. Happiness, she says, is bringing stuffed animals to children in hospitals. And, Michelle believes, happiness comes not from winning but from doing the best that she can!

Career Highlights

- 1998 Winter Olympics, Silver Medal
- U.S. Olympic Committee Athlete of the Month, January 1998
- 1998 U.S. Championship, Gold Medal
- Winner of the 1998 Chevrolet Perfect 6.0 Award
- 1997 Skate Canada, Gold Medal
- Winner of the 1997 Dial Award for Outstanding High School Seniors
- 1997 Skate America, Gold Medal
- 1997 Nice 'N Easy Team Challenge, Silver (top individual scores overall)
- 1997 Honda Prelude Cup, Gold Medal
- U.S. Olympic Committee Athlete of the Month, October 1997
- 1997 Hershey's Kisses Team Challenge, Gold Medal
- 1997 World Championship, Silver Medal
- 1997 ISU Champions Series Final, Silver Medal
- 1997 U.S. Championship, Silver Medal
- 1996 Skate America, Gold Medal
- 1996 Ultimate Four, Gold Medal
- Winner, 1996 Skater of the Year Award, *Skating* magazine (only two-time winner)
- 1996 World Championship, Gold Medal
- 1996 U.S. Championship, Gold Medal
- U.S. Olympic Committee Athlete of the Month, January 1996
- 1996 Trophee Lalique, Gold Medal
- 1996 ISU Champions Series Final, Gold Medal
- 1996 Hershey's Kisses Team Challenge, Gold Medal
- 1996 Continent's Cup, Gold Medal
- 1996 Centennial Cup, Bronze Medal
- *Sports Illustrated For Kids* magazine, Hall of Fame, 1995
- 1995 U.S. Championship, Silver Medal
- 1995 World Championship, Fourth
- 1995 U.S. Team Challenge, Gold Medal
- 1995 Nations Cup, Gold Medal
- 1995 Skate America, Gold Medal
- 1995 Skate Canada, Gold Medal
- 1995 Spring Pro-Am, Gold Medal
- Winner, 1994 Skater of the Year Award, *Skating* magazine
- 1994 U.S. Championship, Silver Medal
- 1994 World Championship, Eighth
- 1994 Ladies Outdoor Challenge, Gold Medal
- 1994 World Junior Championship, Gold Medal
- 1994 Goodwill Games, Silver Medal
- 1994 Skate America, Silver Medal
- 1993 Olympic Festival, Gold Medal
- 1993 Gardena Spring Trophy, Gold Medal
- 1993 Pacific Coast Sectionals, Gold Medal
- 1993 Southwest Pacific Regionals, Gold Medal

Glossary

axel: A difficult jump in which the skater takes off while skating forward, rotates one and one-half turns in the air, and lands on the opposite foot. It is often called "the king of jumps."

choreography: The planning and arrangement of steps and moves in a musical program of the skater's choice.

combination: Two jumps performed in sequence without any footwork or moves in between.

double: Any jump in which the skater turns two rotations in the air before landing.

exhibition: A program used in events and shows that are not judged.

flip: A jump in which the skater takes off from the back inside edge using the opposite skate's toe pick, rotates in the air, and lands backwards on the opposite foot.

free skate: A program set to music lasting approximately four minutes, in which the skater can add any elements including footwork, jumps and spins. Also known as the *long program.*

loop: A jump in which the skater takes off from the back outside edge of the skate, rotates, and lands on the same foot.

lutz: A difficult jump in which the skater takes off

from the back outside edge of the skate blade, using the toe pick of the opposite foot and lands backwards on the opposite foot.

professional: A skater who has given up his or her eligibility for the Olympics.

sit spin: A move in which the skater squats and extends the free leg in front of the body while spinning.

technical program: A routine set to music lasting approximately two minutes, judged on required elements: jumps, spins, and footwork. Also known as the *short program.*

triple: Any jump in which the skater rotates three times in the air before landing.

toe loop: Similar to the loop, except that the skater takes off from the toe pick.

Sources

Information for this book was obtained from the following sources: The Associated Press, AP Report, 17 March 1996; Linda Bao, The Unofficial Michelle Kwan Website, America Online, 1997; Debbie Becker (*USA Today*, 17 July 1997); Marcia Burchstead and Dale Mitch (*Blades On Ice*, May/June 1995); Carol Cain (*Mobile Register*, 17 May 1996); Cam Cole (*Edmonton Journal*, 24 March 1996); Bob Der (*Sports Illustrated for Kids*, February 1995); George Diaz (*The Orlando Sentinel*, 2 February 1994); Ric Dolphin (*Edmonton Journal*, 24 March 1996); Brendan Hanrahan (*Chicago Tribune*, 8 February 1994); Randy Harvey (*Los Angeles Times*, 28 October 1996, 4 January 1994); Phil Hersh (*Chicago Tribune*, 3 February 1994, 7 February 1995, 12 March 1995, 26 November 1995, 14 January 1996, 25 February 1996, 24 March 1996, 10 February 1997); Joanne Ireland (*Edmonton Journal*, 20 March 1996, 23 March 1996); Michelle Kwan, as told to Laura James (*Heart Of A Champion*, 1997); Gil LeBreton (*Fort Worth Star-Telegram*, 11 January 1998); Jere Longman (*The New York Times*, 17 July 1997); Steve Milton (*Super Skaters*, 1997); John Powers (*The Boston Globe Magazine*, 26 January 1997); Marge Reynolds (*Blades On Ice*, July/August 1997); *Minneapolis-St. Paul Star Tribune*, 14 June 1996; Peter Sibbald (*Sports Illustrated for Kids*, Girls and Sports Extra, 1996); *Time for Kids* (2 February 1996); Lynn Zinser (*The Philadelphia Inquirer*, 12 January 1998).

Index

Write to Michelle

You can send mail to Michelle at the address on the right. If you write a letter, don't get your hopes up too high. Michelle and other athletes get lots of letters every day, and they aren't always able to answer them all.

Michelle Kwan
c/o Proper Marketing Associates
44450 Pinetree Drive, Suite 103
Plymouth, MI 48170

Acknowledgments

Photographs reproduced with permission of: © ALLSPORT USA/ Mike Powell, pp. 1, 26; © ALLSPORT USA/Jamie Squire, pp. 38, 57; © ALLSPORT USA/Clive Brunskill, pp. 6, 56; © Kathy Goedeken, pp. 2, 9, 11, 12, 16, 21, 22, 33, 34, 41, 44, 45, 46, 50, 51, 53, 58; © Michelle Harvath, pp. 15, 18; © ALLSPORT USA/Tony Duffy, pp. 25, 29; © ALLSPORT USA/Chris Cole, p. 30; SportsChrome East/West, Rob Tringali Jr., p. 37; © Paul Harvath, p. 43; © ALL-SPORT USA/Doug Pensinger, p. 48; © ALLSPORT USA/Aubrey Washington, p. 54.

Front cover photograph by © ALLSPORT USA/Shaun Botterill.
Back cover photograph by © Paul Harvath.

Artwork by Michael Tacheny.

About the Author

Kimberly Gatto earned her Bachelor of Arts degree with honors from Wheaton College. She is active in several children's charities and teaches horsemanship to young riders.